Eugene, Eugene The Mystery Solving Machine:
Trains Passing By
Activity & Coloring Book

Written by: Dr. Maisha L. Jack

This book is dedicated to my father, Danny Eugene Thomas Sr. For all of your sacrifices, your support, your guidance, your standing in the shadows, and your life's lessons, I thank you.

You are one of the most giving, loving, and inquisitive people that I know. Look more at the achievements than mistakes, for you have stood in the gap of ensuring that your children knew that you were always present. I love you and I am glad to call you my daddy.

Tickets for Trains Passing By

Use the graph to help answer the questions.
Check the correct answer.

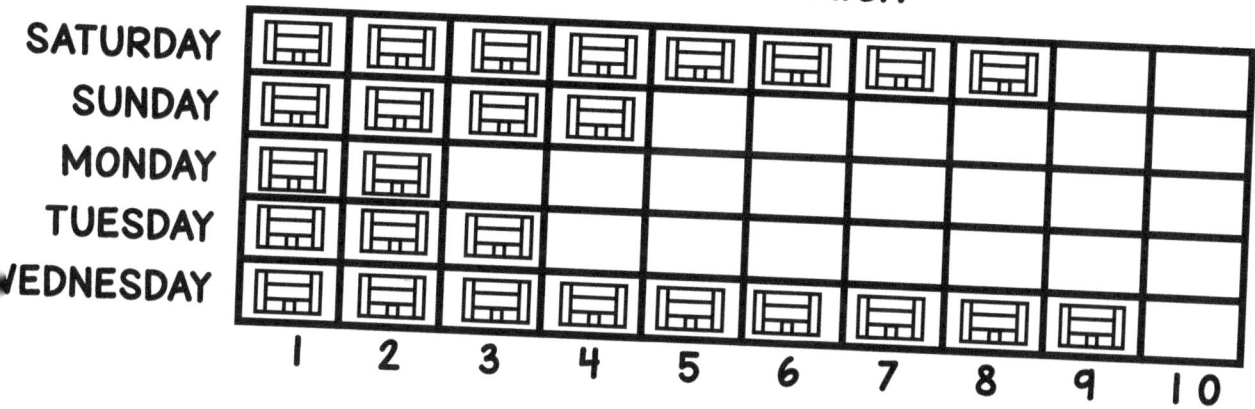

	1	2	3	4	5	6	7	8	9	10
SATURDAY	▢	▢	▢	▢	▢	▢	▢	▢		
SUNDAY	▢	▢	▢	▢						
MONDAY	▢	▢								
TUESDAY	▢	▢	▢							
WEDNESDAY	▢	▢	▢	▢	▢	▢	▢	▢	▢	

1. On which day were the most tickets sold?

☐ SUNDAY   ☐ WEDNESDAY   ☐ SATURDAY

2. How many more tickets were sold on
Wednesday than on Saturday?

1 ☐   4 ☐   7 ☐   3 ☐

3. How many tickets were sold on both
Saturday and Sunday?

10 ☐   12 ☐   11 ☐   8 ☐

Write the missing numbers to complete the number sentence

$2 + \boxed{} = 10$

$4 + \boxed{} = 10$

$6 + \boxed{} = 10$

$8 + \boxed{} = 10$

$9 + \boxed{} = 10$

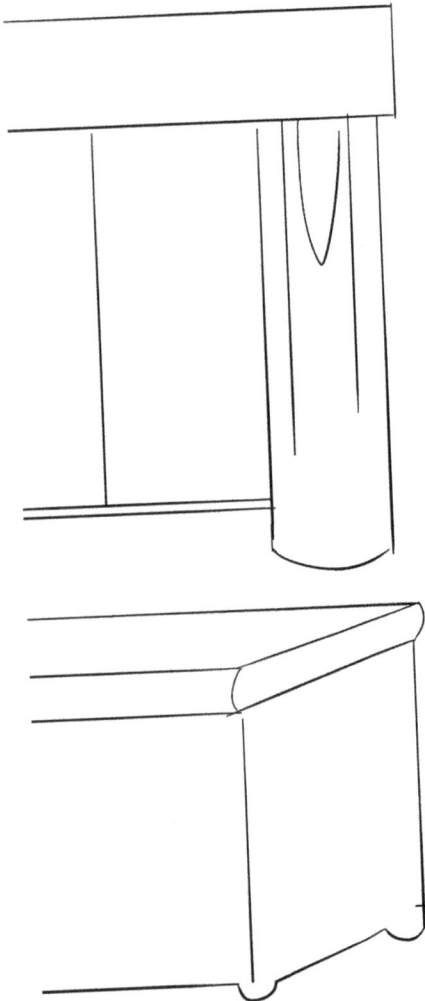

Write the missing numbers to complete the number sentence

$11 - \boxed{} = 10$

$13 - \boxed{} = 10$

$15 - \boxed{} = 10$

$17 - \boxed{} = 10$

$19 - \boxed{} = 10$

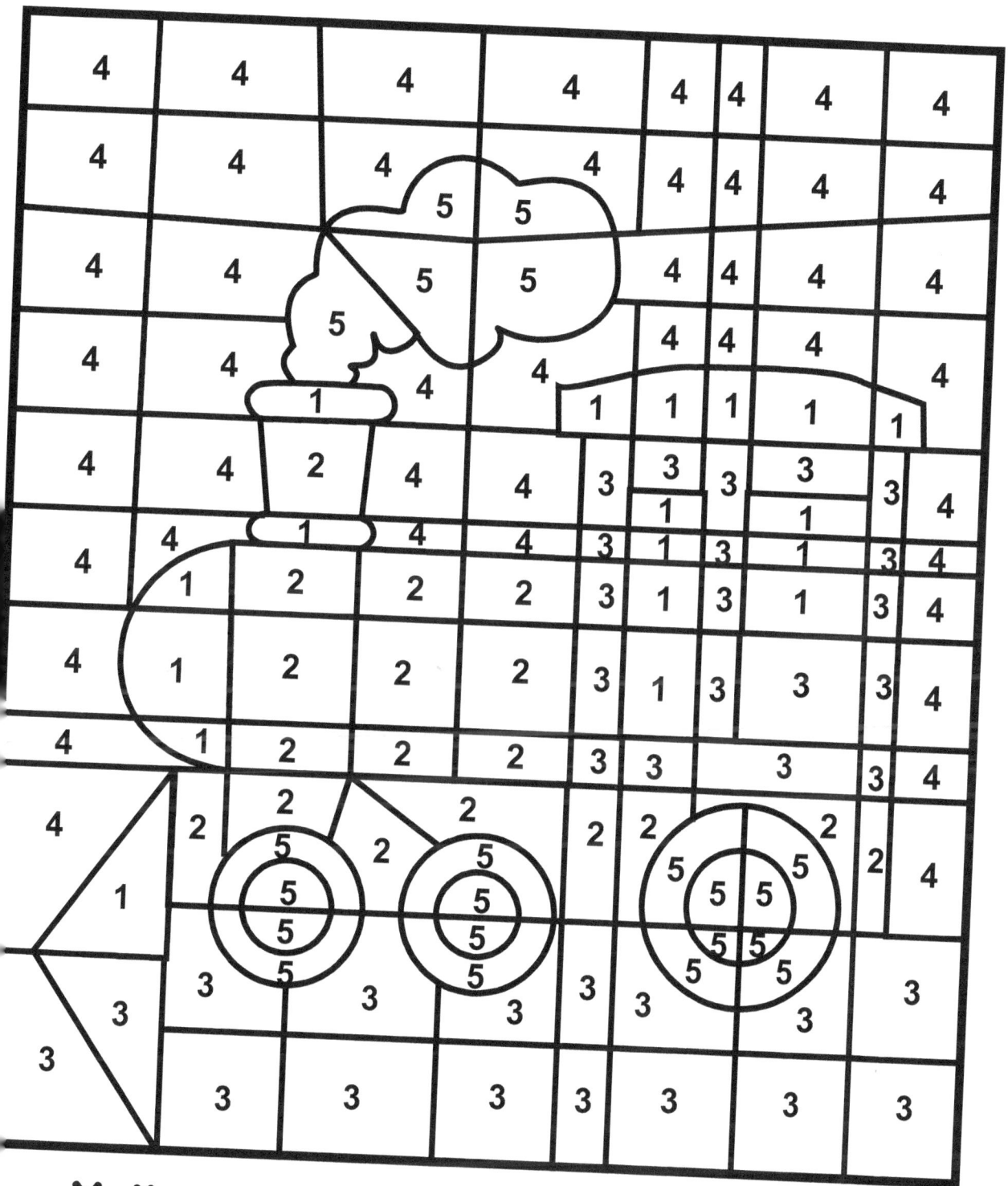

- Yellow   2 - Red   3 - Green
4 - Blue   5 - Black

Positive Affirmations and Strengths

There are many things I am good at. Anytime
I am feeling discouraged, I will think about my
strengths

● I am ...

● I am ...

● I am ...

● I am ...

● I am ...

STRENGTHS
artistic
athletic
a team player
brave

curious
fair
friendly
focused
funny
giving

honest
kind
loving
loyal
organized
respectful
strong

Word Search

```
Q N Z X P J D E T E C T I V E
J F T H L T L P Z N V Z I F G
A F K R E D C K U Y G L S P D
A P W R W O C F A L L Y M H L
N I K S I U A J X P S D Y A M
E U D Z S P R X K A J R S S F
E U G E N E C S R S U M T N R
X S A V W X H F X S W L E V E
Y D R R P K I O B E L M R L I
O E H U W K T R P N U K Y B G
O O Y R D P E O C G Z J R E H
L O U I S E C C Q E V Y P I T
H C S B T L T K U R R U D D P
P T S I G O N D T R A I N V I
J N L D G I X Z L F M P H M L
```

EUGENE
LOUISE
LEWIS
ROCK
FALLY

TRAIN
FREIGHT
PASSENGER
DETECTIVE
MYSTERY
ARCHITECT

Word Search

```
O X Y L X V T V E J C S R J S
G E X P L O R E R S Y A E Z J
Q X A R T I F A C T K R S N A
P U P U C P L E M Z D C F X S
N W Y L O Y P S V L A H J D P
Q X O B N P Z O F Q D A O P H
M C E K Q K Q X B N D E J G A
G O A F U F F W V Z Y O D Z L
P N U N E J K C G I L L Q K T
R D G A R C H A E O L O G Y G
E U U E O U R B X B Z G O R Y
B C S C R T T O Q E Q I Y O W
A T T V Y S I O X N L S A J F
R O P H R D S S S P O T X G I
R R Z M B G C E G B Z T N A O
```

ARCHAEOLOGIST
ARCHAEOLOGY
REBAR
ASPHALT
CABOOSE

CONDUCTOR
CONQUEROR
ARTIFACT
EXPLORERS
AUGUST
DADDY

Re-write each word using capital letters as needed

pearl street	august	catfish	mystery
march	fried potatoes	pet	winchester
may	train	goldfish	kentucky
july	detective	library	leader
april	breakfast	oliver school	tea

Find and circle the hidden objects in this picture.

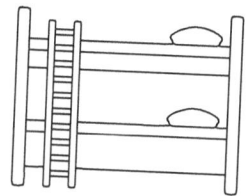

Connect the dots for each character then color

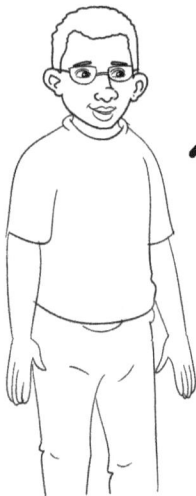

Help Eugene find the Library

www.ingramcontent.com/pod-product-compliance
Lightning Source LLC
Chambersburg PA
CBHW081236020426
42331CB00012B/3203